OECD Skills Studies

The Jobs Again Reform in Greece

OECD CENTRE FOR SKILLS EVALUATIONS

OECD
BETTER POLICIES FOR BETTER LIVES

This work is published under the responsibility of the Secretary-General of the OECD. The opinions expressed and arguments employed herein do not necessarily reflect the official views of the Member countries of the OECD.

This document, as well as any data and map included herein, are without prejudice to the status of or sovereignty over any territory, to the delimitation of international frontiers and boundaries and to the name of any territory, city or area.

Please cite this publication as:
OECD (2025), *The Jobs Again Reform in Greece: OECD Centre for Skills Evaluations*, OECD Skills Studies, OECD Publishing, Paris, https://doi.org/10.1787/bff1cb60-en.

ISBN 978-92-64-84200-7 (print)
ISBN 978-92-64-32934-8 (PDF)
ISBN 978-92-64-85230-3 (HTML)

OECD Skills Studies
ISSN 2307-8723 (print)
ISSN 2307-8731 (online)

Photo credits: Cover © f11photo/Shutterstock.com.

Corrigenda to OECD publications may be found at: https://www.oecd.org/en/publications/support/corrigenda.html.

Foreword

The "Jobs Again" reform represents one of Greece's most ambitious efforts to modernise its approach to vocational education and training. Introduced in 2022, the reform seeks to strengthen the effectiveness, accountability, and labour market relevance of continuous vocational education and training (CVET) by introducing performance-based funding, digital infrastructure, and enhanced provider oversight. As Greece continues to contend with persistent skills mismatches and high unemployment – particularly among young people – it is essential to assess the designed and implementation of these policy measures.

This report, *The Jobs Again Reform in Greece: OECD Centre for Skills Evaluations*, constitutes an independent assessment of the reform's quality assurance mechanisms, focusing on provider accreditation, key performance indicators (KPIs), and institutional co-ordination. The evaluation draws on document analysis, stakeholder interviews, and international comparisons to identify areas for improvement and provide actionable recommendations for policymakers.

The report highlights the need for clearer institutional roles in quality assurance, more flexible and inclusive KPI frameworks, and better alignment between training content and evolving labour market needs. It also underscores the importance of using pre- and post-training assessments to evaluate learning progress, protecting access for vulnerable groups, and ensuring the reliability of certification mechanisms.

While this study focuses on identifying areas for improvement, it also recognises the bold steps taken by Greece to reform its CVET system. The introduction of individual learning accounts, the establishment of a national registry of providers, and the development of a unified digital platform represent significant progress. These efforts can support the creation of a more responsive, efficient, and learner-centered skills system.

The relevance of this evaluation extends beyond Greece. Many countries are experimenting with performance-based funding and digital delivery models in adult learning. By documenting the Greek experience, this report contributes to a broader policy dialogue on how to improve training quality and better connect people with employment opportunities.

The OECD Centre for Skills is committed to supporting countries in evaluating and improving their skills systems. Through rigorous and independent assessments, the Centre helps governments identify practical pathways to reform, ensuring that skills policies remain fit for purpose in a rapidly changing world.

Acknowledgements

The OECD extends its sincere gratitude to the staff of the Greek Public Employment Service (DYPA) for their indispensable contributions to this evaluation. Their active participation in meetings, interviews and consultations was instrumental to the success of the project.

Special thanks are extended to Spiros Protopsaltis, Governor and Chairman of the Board of Directors of DYPA, and Yianna Hormova, Deputy Governor of DYPA, for their leadership and support. The OECD also acknowledges the valuable assistance of Theodoridou Nasia, Laina Evi, Skoura Evi, and Bounova Anastasia, whose efforts in co-ordination, logistics and feedback significantly facilitated the evaluation process.

The OECD further recognises the engagement of representatives from the MEKY Unit of Experts in Employment, Social Insurance, Welfare and Social Affairs, as well as members of the National Skills Council, whose insights were proved highly valuable.

Further appreciation is extended to representatives of the Hellenic Federation of Enterprises (SEV), the General Confederation of Greek Workers, and the Hellenic Accreditation System (ESYD), whose perspectives enriched the analysis. The OECD also acknowledges the meaningful contributions of representatives from the National Organization for the Certification of Qualifications and Vocational Guidance (EOPPEP) and the Ministry of Education, Religious Affairs and Sports.

This report was prepared by Ricardo Espinoza, Laura Reznikova and Abigail Sageev, who served as the OECD project leaders responsible for co-ordinating the evaluation and drafting the analysis.

The OECD gratefully acknowledges the contributions of Stefan Jahnke and Anthony Camilleri of the Knowledge Innovation Centre (KIC), who contributed as external experts to this project. Their analytical input and policy expertise significantly enriched both the overall assessment and the development of the international case studies.

This project was supervised by Andrew Bell, Head of OECD Skills Strategies and Deputy Head of the OECD Centre for Skills, who provided analytical and drafting guidance. Strategic oversight was provided by El Iza Mohamedou, Head of the OECD Centre for Skills; Stefano Scarpetta, OECD Director for Employment, Labour and Social Affairs; and Mark Pearson, OECD Deputy Director for Employment, Labour and Social Affairs.

Further thanks are extended to Hudson Hastings, Yasmeen Shamshoum, and Maria Vaz Pato, interns at the OECD Centre for Skills, for their support in research and co-ordination.

Finally, appreciation is extended to Tara Byrne for her excellent work in mission organisation and to Jennifer Cannon for communication and publication support.

Table of contents

Foreword 3

Acknowledgements 4

Abbreviations and acronyms 7

Executive summary 8

1 Introduction 9
Reference 11

2 Overview of the "Jobs Again" reform 12
Main changes introduced by the reform 13

3 Mapping the "Jobs Again" reform through five key dimensions 17
Ensuring Minimum Standards 18
Ensuring Student Participation in Quality Learning 18
Measuring Training Outcomes and Long-term Impact 18
Performance-based Monitoring 19
Co-ordination and Governance 19

4 Analysis of the "Jobs Again" reform 20
General assessment of the reform's approach 21
Reference 28

5 International case studies: Lessons for Greece 29
Case study 1: Singapore 30
Case study 2: France 33
Case study 3: Austria 34
Case study 4: Estonia 36
References 38
Note 39

6 Conclusions and recommendations for refining the "Jobs Again" reform 40
Dimension 1: Ensuring Minimum Standards 41
Dimension 2: Ensuring Student Participation in Quality Learning 42
Dimension 3: Measuring Training Outcomes and Long-term Impact 43
Dimension 4: Performance-based Monitoring 43

Dimension 5: Co-ordination and Governance 45
References 47

TABLES

Table 4.1. Overview of key performance indicators (KPIs) for provider evaluation 26
Table 6.1. Expanded performance indicators for training effectiveness 44

Abbreviations and acronyms

The following are the main acronyms cited in this report:

Abbreviation/acronym	Full description
ACRA	Accounting and Corporate Regulatory Authority (Singapore)
ACLP	Advanced Certificate in Learning and Performance
ACTA	Advanced Certificate in Training and Assessment
AMS	Austrian Public Employment Service (Arbeitsmarktservice)
AQ	Austrian Quality Assurance Agency
CCP	Career Conversion Programme (Singapore)
CPF	Compte Personnel de Formation (France)
CVET	Continuous vocational education and training
DAC	Development Assistance Committee (OECD)
DYPA	Greek Public Employment Service (Δημόσια Υπηρεσία Απασχόλησης)
EDB	Economic Development Board (Singapore)
EIPA	European Institute of Public Administration
EOPPEP	National Organisation for the Certification of Qualifications and Vocational Guidance (Greece)
EQAVET	European Quality Assurance in Vocational Education and Training
EQF	European Qualifications Framework
ESF	European Social Fund
ESYD	Hellenic Accreditation System
HA KA	Estonian Quality Agency for Education
ILA	Individual learning account
ILAs	Individual learning accounts
ISO	International Organization for Standardization
JUHAN	Estonian Adult Learning Data System
KIC	Knowledge Innovation Centre
KPI	Key performance indicator
KPIs	Key performance indicators
MEKY	Unit of Experts in Employment, Social Insurance, Welfare & Social Affairs (Greece)
MOE	Ministry of Education
MTI	Ministry of Trade and Industry (Singapore)
NSC	National Skills Council (Greece)
OBE	Outcome-Based Education
OECD	Organisation for Economic Co-operation and Development
OR	Organisation Registration (SkillsFuture Singapore process)
OSKA	Labour-Market Monitoring and Forecasting System (Estonia)
RTP	Registered Training Provider (Singapore)
SCTP	SkillsFuture Career Transition Programme
SEV	Hellenic Federation of Enterprises
SSG	SkillsFuture Singapore
TRAQOM	Training Quality and Outcomes Measurement
VET	Vocational education and training
WIFI	Wirtschaftsförderungsinstitut (Austria)
WSQ	Workforce Skills Qualifications (Singapore)
WSP	Work-Study Programme (Singapore)

Executive summary

Greece's "Jobs Again" reform marks a strategically important step toward strengthening the country's continuous vocational education and training (CVET). It introduces a more structured and accountable framework for CVET, aligning public investment with clear expectations around quality, relevance, and outcomes. Through the establishment of a national registry of eligible training providers, the introduction of performance-based funding, and the roll-out of individual learning accounts (ILAs), the reform creates the institutional foundations for a more effective and learner-centered CVET system. These measures represent a deliberate shift towards a model that prioritises results, transparency and responsiveness to labour market needs.

This evaluation by the OECD Centre for Skills examines the quality assurance mechanisms embedded in the reform, with a particular focus on their potential to improve training quality and ensure that public resources are directed towards programmes with demonstrable labour market value. Several positive features are noteworthy. It places greater emphasis on employability outcomes by adopting employment and job retention rates as key performance indicators (KPIs). The reform introduces ISO quality standards as part of the eligibility requirements for training providers, thereby a baseline for institutional capacity. Furthermore, the reform envisages the development of a unified digital platform to facilitate information sharing, enhance access to training opportunities, and support system monitoring. In parallel, the introduction of individual learning accounts (ILAs) enables individuals to select and finance training more directly, within a structured and transparent framework.

Nonetheless, the report identifies several persistent challenges that could constrain the reform's effectiveness if left unaddressed. A key concern is the strong reliance on post-training employment outcomes as a proxy for training quality, since securing a job does not necessarily mean that the training content was relevant or aligned with labour market needs. In the absence of structured pre-training assessments, it remains difficult to measure skills progression or calibrate expectations based on learners' starting points. In addition, the dual-layered quality assurance system – shared between DYPA and EOPPEP – risks producing fragmented oversight, inconsistent enforcement, and avoidable administrative complexity. The current provider evaluation system also offers limited public information, which may hinder learners' ability to make fully informed choices and constrain external scrutiny of provider performance. Lastly, persistently high certification rates raise concerns regarding the rigour and credibility of existing assessment and validation practices.

The report draws on international case studies and stakeholder input to provide practical recommendations for strengthening the implementation of the reform. Clarifying institutional roles, improving support for learners, and refining performance monitoring mechanisms could contribute to a more consistent and effective system. These improvements would enable Greece to build on the progress already made and advance towards a more inclusive and results-oriented CVET system.

1 Introduction

This chapter introduces the context and rationale for Greece's reform of its continuous vocational education and training (CVET) system. It highlights ongoing challenges, including skills mismatches, quality control, challenges, and the underutilisation of performance data. The chapter situates the reform within broader national and European Union (EU) policy priorities, such as reducing unemployment and supporting the digital and green transitions. It also outlines the OECD's evaluation objectives, focusing on the reform's potential to improve training relevance, efficiency, and outcomes, and sets the foundation for the subsequent analysis of quality assurance mechanisms, international comparisons, and policy recommendations.

The continuous vocational education and training (CVET) system in Greece has historically played a crucial role in helping individuals acquire new skills, upskill, or reskill in response to evolving labour market needs. CVET programmes, which are typically designed for adults, offer training that enhances employability, improves career prospects, and facilitates career transitions. They serve a wide range of participants, including unemployed individuals, employees seeking to advance in their careers, and those re-entering the workforce.

However, despite its importance, the Greek CVET system has faced several challenges in recent years. One of the key issues has been the disconnect between training programmes and the real needs of the labour market. Many of the CVET programmes currently being offered are not closely aligned with sectors experiencing skill shortages or emerging industries, which has contributed to a skills mismatch and limited job opportunities for participants after completing their training. Additionally, there are concerns regarding the quality and effectiveness of the training provided, with insufficient mechanisms in place to evaluate the performance of both the training providers and the programmes themselves. As OECD (2024[1]) underscores, robust quality assurance in adult education and training is vital for ensuring that these programmes truly address skill gaps, deliver meaningful returns for learners and the broader economy, and foster greater trust in the overall adult learning system.

Another significant challenge is the lack of accountability and transparency within the CVET system. Public funds are often allocated to training providers without clear performance criteria, and there are limited measures in place to assess whether the training results in tangible outcomes, such as improved employability or job placement. This practice, which does not provide adequate incentives for providers to improve the quality of their programmes, has led to inefficiencies in the use of resources. In addition, the CVET system lacks digital infrastructure to effectively manage and track training data, making it difficult to monitor participants' progress and outcomes.

Recognising these challenges, the Greek government introduced a comprehensive reform under Law 4921/2022, known as "Jobs Again". This reform seeks to overhaul the CVET system to better align it with the current and future demands of the labour market, enhance the quality of training, and improve the overall efficiency of the system.

The reform takes place in a broader context of socio-economic transformation in Greece. The country has faced persistently high unemployment rates, especially among younger workers, and a growing need to modernise its workforce in response to the digital and green transitions. These challenges have been further exacerbated by the COVID-19 pandemic, which accelerated changes in the labour market, highlighting the need for greater flexibility and adaptability in vocational training. Additionally, Greece's efforts to align its policies with European Union objectives on skills development and lifelong learning provided further incentives for the reform. The reform responds directly to EU initiatives that emphasise the need for digital and green skills, as well as the importance of continuous learning throughout people's career.

In summary, the reform of the CVET system in Greece is taking place within the context of persistent unemployment, skills mismatches, and the need to adapt to technological advancements and global economic changes. The reform represents a significant effort to modernise the country's vocational training infrastructure, making it more responsive to labour market demands and ensuring that participants acquire the skills necessary to thrive in a rapidly changing economy.

The OECD has conducted an evaluation of the "Jobs Again" reform with the aim of identifying areas for improvement that could strengthen the reform's contribution to Greece's skills system. The focus of this evaluation is to assess the quality assurance mechanisms introduced by the reform, particularly in the relation to performance-based accountability, oversight of training providers, and alignment with the labour market. While recognising the broad scope of the reform, the report concentrates on key dimensions that are critical to its capacity to improve training quality and support effective upskilling and reskilling.

This report draws on the OECD's international expertise in skills, VET and adult learning systems and is based on document analysis, structured interviews with key stakeholders, and a comparative review of international practices. It offers an independent and evidence-based assessment of the reform's design and early implementation. Chapter 2 outlines the main features of the reform, including the modernisation of the Greek Public Employment Service (DYPA) and the introduction of a digitalised, performance-based funding model. Chapter 3 introduces the five-dimension framework used to assess the reform and guide the analysis. Chapter 4 provides a detailed assessment of the reform's quality assurance mechanisms across five core dimensions. Chapter 5 offers international case studies to contextualise the Greek approach, and Chapter 6 presents targeted recommendations to strengthen implementation and improve alignment with labour market needs.

Reference

OECD (2024), *Quality Matters: Strengthening the Quality Assurance of Adult Education and Training*, OECD Skills Studies, OECD Publishing, Paris, https://doi.org/10.1787/f44a185b-en. [1]

2 Overview of the "Jobs Again" reform

This chapter outlines the main features of Greece's continuous vocational education and training (CVET) reform introduced under the 2022 "Jobs Again" law. It highlights major policy changes designed to enhance quality, accountability, and alignment with labour market needs, including the establishment of individual learning accounts, the adoption of a performance-based funding model, and the rollout of a digital management platform. The chapter also describes the creation of a national registry of eligible training providers, underpinned by rigorous eligibility criteria and outcome-based evaluations. Together, these measures aim to modernise the CVET system, promote transparency, and ensure that public funds support high-impact training aligned with the evolving needs of the Greek economy.

The "Jobs Again" reform aims to modernise DYPA, Greece's Public Employment Service, and strengthen its management of continuous vocational education and training (CVET) programmes to achieve tangible results such as boosting employability and addressing key skills gaps.

To achieve these goals, the reform introduces measures to enhance the quality of CVET, emphasising transparency, accountability, and alignment with labour market requirements.

A key feature of the reform is the introduction of a performance-based accountability framework. This framework ensures that training providers are held accountable for the outcomes they deliver, with regular evaluations based on key performance indicators such as employment rates, participant satisfaction, and employer feedback, rather than traditional input measures like course duration. By linking funding to performance, the reform aims to improve the overall quality and effectiveness of the training programmes offered.

Transparency and accountability will be further strengthened by setting clear eligibility standards for training providers, including certifications such as ISO 9001 for quality management and ISO 27001 for data security. Providers will undergo regular evaluations to maintain these standards, with non-compliance leading to potential removal from the registry of approved providers.

The reform also seeks to ensure that CVET programmes are aligned with the real needs of the labour market. In collaboration with the National Skills Council, the Public Employment Service (DYPA) will conduct regular analyses of labour market trends and skill shortages. This will help to ensure that training programmes are not only relevant but also adaptable to the shifting demands of the economy. For example, particular emphasis will be placed on training in digital and green skills, reflecting the growing importance of these areas in both the Greek and global labour markets. By aligning training with current and future labour market needs, the reform aims to reduce unemployment and underemployment while supporting economic growth.

A significant innovation introduced by the reform is the creation of individual learning accounts for all participants seeking training under subsidised programmes. These accounts will allow individuals to accumulate subsidised training rights over time, giving them the flexibility to choose training that best suits their career development needs. Managed through a digital platform, these accounts will ensure that participants have full transparency regarding their training entitlements, helping them make informed decisions about their education and career progression. This platform will also facilitate the management of training, consulting, and certification services, ensuring that participants can easily access the services they need.

Finally, the reform seeks to improve the overall management and efficiency of the CVET system by leveraging digital technologies. A new digital platform will be developed to manage the entire training process, from registration and course delivery to certification and post-training follow-up. This platform will enable seamless data exchange between training providers, participants, and government agencies, ensuring that the system is both efficient and transparent. Additionally, the platform will allow for real-time tracking of training outcomes, enabling continuous monitoring and evaluation of the effectiveness of CVET programmes. This will help to ensure that public funds are used efficiently, and that the system as a whole is responsive to the needs of both participants and the economy.

Main changes introduced by the reform

The Law 4921/2022 introduces a series of significant changes designed to overhaul the continuous vocational education and training (CVET) system in Greece. The primary objectives of these changes are to enhance the quality of training programmes, strengthen accountability, and ensure better alignment with the evolving needs of the labour market. These reforms are backed by a comprehensive regulatory framework, ensuring structured implementation. The combination of individualised learner funding, digital monitoring tools, and outcome-based provider management represents a forward-looking and innovative approach to CVET reform aimed at enhancing effectiveness, transparency, and accountability. Below is a detailed explanation of the key changes introduced by the reform.

Creation of individual learning accounts (ILAs)

A major innovation introduced by the reform is the establishment of individual learning accounts for all participants seeking training under subsidised programmes. These accounts are designed to give beneficiaries control over their training opportunities and ensure that they have access to relevant, high-quality programmes that match their career aspirations.

Participants can use these accounts to:

- Accumulate training rights over time, allowing them to access additional training as needed throughout their careers. This flexible approach ensures that individuals can continue to upskill and reskill in line with changing labour market demands.
- Select providers from the national registry, ensuring that they can choose high-quality training programmes that meet their specific needs.
- Track their progress through a digital platform, which integrates with the broader management system established by DYPA. This platform provides real-time information on the availability of courses, the progress of participants, and the outcomes of their training.

The introduction of individual learning accounts is part of a broader effort to modernise the management of CVET programmes and to ensure that participants have full transparency and control over their educational and career development.

Integration of labour market needs into training programmes

Under the reform, all subsidised CVET programmes must be aligned with the current and future needs of the labour market. This alignment is achieved through regular labour market analyses, conducted by DYPA in collaboration with the National Skills Council. These analyses help identify emerging skill gaps and areas of high demand in the economy, particularly in fields related to digital transformation and green technologies.

Providers are expected to design and deliver training programmes that address these skill shortages, ensuring that participants are equipped with the knowledge and abilities necessary to succeed in the evolving labour market. Failure to align training with market demands can result in providers losing their eligibility for subsidies, further reinforcing the focus on outcomes and relevance.

Digitalisation of the CVET system

The reform places a strong emphasis on the digitalisation of the CVET system. A new digital platform will be developed to manage all aspects of the training process, from provider registration and course delivery to post-training follow-up and certification. This platform will:

- Streamline the administrative processes for both providers and participants, reducing bureaucracy and improving the efficiency of the system.
- Enable real-time data exchange between training providers, participants, and DYPA, ensuring that all stakeholders have access to up-to-date information on training programmes and outcomes.
- Provide participants with a user-friendly interface to manage their individual learning accounts, track their progress, and access relevant training opportunities.

This digital infrastructure is designed to support the reform's broader goal of improving transparency, accountability, and efficiency within the CVET system. By leveraging technology, the Greek government aims to create a more responsive and flexible training system that can quickly adapt to the changing needs of the labour market.

Creation of the Registry of Eligible Providers

One of the most important changes is the establishment of a Registry of Eligible Providers for subsidised CVET programmes under the new ILA scheme. This registry is created in accordance with Article 37 of Law 4921/2022 and is a crucial element of the new quality assurance system.

Under the new reform, all training providers will need to undergo an initial licensing process overseen by EOPPEP (National Organisation for the Certification of Qualifications and Vocational Guidance), which operates under the Ministry of Education. This accreditation process, based on the national quality assurance framework for vocational education and training, will serve as the first quality filter for training providers.

In addition to this requirement, training providers must meet a set of eligibility criteria that are rigorously defined in the regulation FEK B 3703/2022. These criteria ensure that only providers with a proven track record of delivering high-quality training are allowed to participate in subsidised programmes.

The eligibility requirements include:

- **Quality certifications:** Providers must have certifications such as ISO 9001:2015 (Quality Management Systems) to demonstrate their ability to manage and deliver high-quality training programmes. Additionally, they must hold ISO 27001:2013 (Information Security Management) to ensure that data handling and privacy are managed securely.
- **Capability requirements:** Providers must have the capacity to deliver e-learning, blended learning, and traditional in-person training. They must demonstrate the ability to create educational content, train instructors, manage practical training, and follow-up with trainees post-programme to ensure the effectiveness of the training.
- **Data management and monitoring:** Providers must maintain a comprehensive system for tracking participants, including their progress and outcomes, ensuring transparency and accountability in the training process. This system must integrate with the broader digital infrastructure established by the reform to allow real-time monitoring of the programmes.

Providers are also subject to continuous evaluation. Those that fail to meet performance standards may be removed from the registry, losing their eligibility to offer subsidised training. This approach ensures that only high-performing providers remain in the system, raising the overall quality of training available to participants.

Removal from the Registry

Building on the initial accreditation process, DYPA will establish a Registry of Eligible Providers for subsidised CVET programmes. Admission to this registry will require providers not only to be accredited by EOPPEP but also to comply with performance-based quality criteria set by DYPA. These criteria are designed to ensure that public funding is allocated to providers that effectively prepare participants for the labour market.

The reform introduces a performance-based funding model, where providers are evaluated against specific key performance indicators (KPIs). These indicators prioritise labour market outcomes, programme quality, and stakeholder satisfaction. Providers who fail to meet at least three of the five core KPIs (see below) will be removed from the registry for two years, losing eligibility for public funding. If, after this period, they reapply and continue to underperform, they will face an additional two-year removal.

Key performance indicators (KPIs) and conditions for removal

Providers will be assessed based on the following KPIs:

1. **Employment Rate:** At least 50% of unemployed trainees must secure employment within 12 months of programme completion.
2. **Job Retention:** At least 90% of trained workers must remain employed for a minimum of 12 months post-training.
3. **Participant Satisfaction**: At least 75% of trainees must evaluate the programme positively, based on post-training surveys.
4. **Employer Satisfaction**: At least 75% of employers engaged in training programmes must provide positive feedback.
5. **Certification Rate**: At least 80% of trainees who complete the programme must obtain a formal certification.

3 Mapping the "Jobs Again" reform through five key dimensions

This chapter presents the five-dimension framework used to assess Greece's "Jobs Again" reform in continuing vocational education and training (CVET). The framework comprises: 1) Ensuring Minimum Standards, 2) Ensuring Student Participation in Quality Learning, 3) Measuring Training Outcomes and Long-term Impact, 4) Performance-based Monitoring and 5) Co-ordination and Governance. Together, these dimensions enable a comprehensive evaluation of training quality, effectiveness, and system coherence. They also serve as a reference for international case studies and inform the report's policy recommendations aimed at strengthening the performance and accountability of Greece's CVET system.

This report applies a five-dimension framework to assess Greece's "Jobs Again" reform and identify areas for improvement in its continuing vocational education and training (CVET) system. This framework enables a comprehensive analysis of all stages of the training process – from initial accreditation to sustained labour market outcomes – and will be applied not only in assessing the reform but also in guiding international case studies and formulating policy recommendations. The sections below summarise each dimension of the framework.

Ensuring Minimum Standards

This dimension focuses on maintaining baseline quality across training providers to ensure consistency and effectiveness. It sets the foundation for the entire CVET system by establishing the basic requirements that providers must meet in order to receive state funding and deliver training programmes. Key elements include:

- **Licensing Requirements**: Providers must meet regional or national licensing criteria to operate, ensuring that they adhere to fundamental quality benchmarks.
- **Access to State-funded Programmes**: Providers seeking public funding are subject to additional eligibility criteria, helping maintain a consistent level of service quality.
- **Performance-based Incentives**: Reward and compensation schemes are tied to measurable performance, incentivising providers to deliver high-quality training in line with public objectives.

Ensuring Student Participation in Quality Learning

The second dimension emphasises the content, delivery, and monitoring of training, placing learner needs at the centre of the system. It highlights the importance of enrolment assessments, rigorous teaching practices, and continuous oversight. Key elements include:

- **Student Enrolment and Assessment**: Providers conduct pre-training assessments to ensure the right learner is matched to the right programme.
- **Course Delivery Standards**: Training institutions adhere to guidelines on instructional methods and expected learning outcomes.
- **Ongoing Monitoring**: Continuous evaluation of the learning process to confirm that participants are acquiring relevant skills.

Measuring Training Outcomes and Long-term Impact

Dimension three goes beyond immediate training indicators and looks at how well programmes prepare learners for sustainable careers. This perspective draws attention to long-term performance measures such as employment retention and career progression. Key elements include:

- **Certification and Feedback**: Official certifications and participant satisfaction surveys provide short-term indicators of success.
- **Independent Evaluations**: Post-training assessments track skill development, employment outcomes, and workforce integration.
- **Long-term Impact**: Continued follow-up to ensure that training programmes remain aligned with evolving labour market requirements.

Performance-based Monitoring

This dimension emphasises the link between tangible outcomes and funding or recognition, holding providers accountable for their results. It builds upon the foundations set in Dimensions 1, 2, and 3, rewarding effective training and signalling areas needing improvement. Key elements include:

- **Linking Funding to Performance**: Financial support is contingent on concrete outcomes, encouraging providers to maintain high standards.
- **Outcome Metrics**: Key performance indicators (KPIs) focus on employment rates, skill gains, and participant satisfaction, among other measures.
- **Ongoing Monitoring**: Regular reviews of short- and long-term data ensure that providers continuously meet required benchmarks.

Co-ordination and Governance

The fifth dimension addresses how well institutions work together to implement policy, oversee quality, and drive system-wide improvements. It ensures there is no duplication or fragmentation in responsibilities, and that the entire CVET landscape functions as a coherent whole. Key elements include:

- **Institutional Alignment**: Defining the roles of regulatory bodies such as DYPA (Greece's Public Employment Service) and the Ministry of Education to minimise overlap.
- **Stakeholder Engagement**: Collaborating with employers, industry representatives, and social partners to keep training relevant.
- **Cross-Sector Collaboration**: Co-ordinating among education institutions, employment services, and government agencies to support seamless learner transitions from training to work.
- **Accountability and Oversight**: Establishing transparent performance monitoring procedures to ensure goals are consistently met.
- **Data Integration**: Creating real-time data-sharing systems to track learners' progress and labour market outcomes.

4 Analysis of the "Jobs Again" reform

This chapter assesses the quality assurance mechanisms introduced under Greece's "Jobs Again" reform using the five-dimension assessment framework. It analyses DYPA's approach to accrediting and monitoring training providers, with a particular attention to performance-based funding, key performance indicators (KPIs), and the new registry of eligible providers. The chapter highlights strengths, such as increased accountability, while also well as identifying risks related to labour market volatility, equity, and co-ordination challenges between DYPA and existing institutions. The analysis informs recommendations to strengthen the reform's coherence, effectiveness, and alignment with long-term skills development goals.

This chapter provides an assessment of the "Jobs Again" reform, focusing specifically on its quality assurance mechanisms through the lens of the five-dimension framework introduced earlier. The analysis examines the measures that DYPA (Greece's Public Employment Service) is set to implement to accredit and monitor training providers, with particular attention to the introduction of a registry of eligible providers and the use of key performance indicators (KPIs) to ensure accountability and quality.

The assessment offers a general evaluation of the reform's approach using the five dimensions – covering baseline standards, learner experience, outcome measurement, performance-based monitoring, and co-ordination/governance.

While the reform introduces broader changes to Greece's continuous vocational education and training (CVET) system, this evaluation focuses solely on the quality assurance mechanisms that DYPA will implement, particularly those related to provider performance and regulatory oversight.

General assessment of the reform's approach

Dimension 1: Ensuring Minimum Standards

The "Jobs Again" reform represents a fundamental shift in the governance of CVET by introducing performance-based accountability as a core principle. This shift is significant in at least two key ways:

- **Outcome-based evaluation:** The reform moves away from traditional input-based measures (such as course duration or funding per participant) towards an approach that prioritises measurable outcomes, particularly labour market integration.
- **Provider accountability:** The introduction of a registry of eligible providers, combined with strict accreditation and performance monitoring criteria, creates a structured framework to ensure that only high-quality training institutions participate in publicly funded CVET programmes.

These elements align with international trends in skills development, particularly efforts seen in OECD countries to enhance training effectiveness through data-driven decision-making and performance-based funding models. However, successful implementation will depend on the robustness of data collection and enforcement mechanisms.

Additionally, the reform introduces new quality requirements that affect the baseline standards for provider eligibility, including ISO 9001 (Quality Management) and ISO 27001 (Data Security) certifications. While ISO 9001's emphasis on customer satisfaction aligns with general service quality principles, it may be less suitable for a vocational training context where the focus should be on broader external outcomes, such as labour market integration and social impact. Alternative standards such as ISO 21001 (Management Systems for Educational Organisations), ISO 29990 (Learning Services for Non-Formal Education and Training), and ISO 29993 (Learning Services Outside Formal Education) offer more tailored frameworks that focus specifically on educational quality, learner outcomes, and instructional effectiveness. A more detailed assessment is needed to determine which standard – or combination of standards – would best support the reform's objectives in setting minimum requirements.

Dimension 2: Ensuring Student Participation in Quality Learning

A key issue of the current reform is that provider accreditation and evaluation rely primarily on post-training indicators, such as employment rates, job retention, and certification completion (see the following section for a detailed analysis). While these indicators are useful for assessing training effectiveness, they do not guarantee that the training content itself is relevant to current and future skill demands. The reform does not specify how course content will be validated against evolving labour market needs or whether providers must follow a structured framework, such as a national qualifications framework, to ensure consistency in skill classification, competency levels, and alignment with industry standards.

Furthermore, relying on EOPPEP's accreditation of training providers places the responsibility for ensuring quality at the institutional level rather than at the course level. The introduction of individual learning accounts (ILAs) enhances learner choice, but without strong quality control measures for course content, there is no clear safeguard to ensure that the training offered remains relevant and responsive to shifts in labour market demand.

Finally, it is unclear how the reform ensures that training provision is aligned with labour market demands, as the mechanisms for validating training content are not sufficiently defined. The "Jobs Again" reform seeks to align training provision with labour market needs through collaboration with the National Skills Council and use of on sector-based skills forecasts under the updated Skills Strategy (2023). However, the reform does not establish a clear mechanism to ensure that these learning outcomes are consistently aligned to labour market demands. An in-depth analysis of the link between training and the labour market can be found in Output 2: *Policy Analytical Proposal for Greece's 2025 "Strategy for Labour Force Upskilling and Connection to the Labour Market"*

Dimension 3: Measuring Training Outcomes and Long-term Impact

The "Jobs Again" reform places a strong emphasis on post-training outcomes as the primary measure of training effectiveness, relying on what it is known as Outcome-based Education (OBE) principles. However, it lacks a structured pre-training skills assessment, meaning that there is no clear baseline against which to compare post-training progress. This absence of a reference point creates significant challenges in evaluating the true impact of training on participants' skills and employability.

One of the key issues is that training participants are not a homogenous group. For example, the training needs and learning progress of long-term unemployed individuals will differ substantially from those of high-skilled workers seeking upskilling opportunities. Without an initial skills assessment, it becomes difficult to distinguish whether post-training employment outcomes are the result of the training itself or merely a reflection of differences in participants' pre-existing skill levels.

This lack of a baseline also complicates equity in provider evaluation. If performance-based funding and provider accreditation are determined primarily by employment rates and job retention metrics, training centres that work with more disadvantaged or lower-skilled participants may be unfairly penalised compared to those that train already highly employable workers. Without pre-training assessment data, it is difficult to adjust performance expectations based on the initial skills and labour market position of trainees.

Dimension 4: Performance-based Monitoring

The "Jobs Again" reform introduces a performance-based evaluation system for training providers, using key performance indicators (KPIs) to measure training effectiveness. These KPIs serve as benchmarks for determining whether training leads to successful employment outcomes, programme completion, participant satisfaction, and employer engagement. While the reform's emphasis on measurable results is an important step toward improving accountability, each KPI presents unique strengths and limitations that must be carefully considered. This section provides a detailed analysis of each proposed indicator.

1. **Employment Rate**

The employment rate KPI requires that at least 50% of unemployed trainees secure employment within 12 months of completing the programme. This indicator is intended to measure the effectiveness of training in improving employability and is a central metric in evaluating provider performance. By assessing whether participants transition into jobs, it provides a direct measure of labour market integration.

One of the main strengths of this KPI is its clarity and ease of communication. Employment rates are widely understood by policymakers, employers, and the public, making it an accessible metric for assessing the success of vocational training programmes. Additionally, by focusing on employment outcomes rather than training inputs, this KPI encourages providers to align their programmes with real job opportunities, ensuring that the skills being taught are relevant to the labour market.

However, the employment rate KPI is highly dependent on external labour market conditions, making it an imprecise measure of provider quality and effectiveness. Economic downturns, regional disparities in job availability, and fluctuations in demand for skilled workers across different industries all influence employment outcomes independently of the quality of training provided. A high-quality training programme cannot create jobs where they do not exist, and providers working in high-unemployment regions may struggle to meet this target, even if they deliver high-quality instruction. For example, in areas where job opportunities are scarce, factors such as weak local industry, limited employer demand, or economic stagnation can prevent even well-trained graduates from securing employment. This places providers in disadvantaged regions at an inherent disadvantage compared to those in more economically dynamic areas, as their success rate in placing trainees depends as much on external job market conditions as on the effectiveness of their training programmes.

Another limitation of this KPI is its short-term focus. While securing employment within 12 months is an important milestone, it does not account for job quality, career stability, or skill utilisation. Participants may find temporary, low-wage, or part-time jobs that do not fully utilise their training, yet still count towards the KPI. This means that a programme could appear successful on paper despite its graduates being underemployed, working in roles that do not match their newly acquired skills or offer limited career advancement opportunities. For instance, in a tight labour market with widespread shortages, any training may appear effective based on this KPI alone, as employers are willing to hire quickly, even if the match between skills and job requirements is weak. Conversely, in a weaker labour market, even high-quality, demand-driven training may seem ineffective due to limited job opportunities. The risk in the latter scenario is that if this KPI is used to justify discontinuing programmes that fail to meet short-term employment targets, it could lead to long-term skill shortages once the labour market recovers.

Additionally, there is a risk of selection bias, where providers may prioritise trainees who are easier to place in jobs – such as individuals with higher existing qualifications or work experience – while neglecting more vulnerable groups, including long-term unemployed individuals, migrants, or workers with disabilities. If providers are primarily evaluated on employment outcomes, they may avoid serving those who face structural barriers to employment, thereby reinforcing rather than reducing existing inequalities.

2. **Job Retention**

The job retention KPI requires that at least 90% of trained workers must remain employed for at least 12 months after securing a job. This indicator aims to measure the sustainability of employment outcomes, ensuring that trainees are not just placed in jobs but are able to maintain employment over time.

A key advantage of this KPI is that it introduces a longer-term perspective on employment quality. Unlike the employment rate, which only considers whether a participant finds a job, job retention provides insight into whether that job is stable. This helps distinguish between short-term job placements and meaningful career opportunities, making it a stronger indicator of workforce integration.

However, despite its focus on employment sustainability, this KPI does not measure career progression or skill utilisation. A participant may remain employed for 12 months, but in a job that does not require the skills acquired through training. Without data on wage growth, promotions, or skill utilisation, the job retention KPI will not capture whether training has led to actual career advancement.

Furthermore, job retention is influenced by external factors beyond the provider's control. Some industries experience high turnover rates due to seasonal employment, contractual limitations, or economic shifts. Even a well-trained worker may be laid off due to business restructuring or automation, making this KPI an unreliable measure of training quality in certain sectors. This is especially true in trades and industries with cyclical employment patterns, where frequent periods of unemployment are the norm rather than a sign of inadequate training. For example, in tourism-related sectors, where many jobs are concentrated in the peak summer season, followed by months of inactivity. This inherent seasonality not only distorts job retention metrics, making them less reliable, but also deters potential workers from pursuing careers in these fields. As a result, employers may face persistent labour shortages, exacerbated by the unattractive nature of these roles due to the downtime.

Like the employment rate, this KPI can disadvantage providers working with vulnerable groups. Participants with precarious work histories or gaps in employment may face higher job instability, making it more difficult for providers to meet retention targets. As a result, providers may focus on trainees who are already more likely to retain employment, further exacerbating selection bias.

3. **Certification Rate**

Once participants complete their training, their skills are certified by third-party certifiers. Certifiers are informed of a programme's schedule once it begins, including its expected completion date. Participants can choose from one to two designated certifiers per programme to validate their skills. These certifiers operate under the supervision of the Ministry of Development, while the CVET providers are overseen by the National Organisation for the Certification of Qualifications and Vocational Guidance (EOPPEP), under the Ministry of Education. DYPA also conducts spontaneous audits to verify programme delivery and compliance with its requirements.

The certification rate KPI mandates that at least 80% of trainees who complete the programme must obtain certification. This indicator is based on the assumption that certification represents a meaningful measure of skills acquisition, providing formal recognition of training outcomes.

A major strength of this KPI is that it encourages programme completion and ensures that participants receive documented proof of their skills, which can be useful for job applications. It also promotes standardisation within the vocational training system by requiring providers to meet clear certification benchmarks.

However, certification does not necessarily guarantee employability. Many workers with certifications still struggle to find jobs if their newly acquired skills are not in demand. The labour market value of a certificate depends on whether employers recognise and trust the credential, as well as whether the skills being certified match industry needs.

Another issue is that certification pass rates are already between 90-100% in many cases, meaning that this KPI may not differentiate high-quality training from ineffective programmes, raising concerns about the integrity of the certification process and the quality of outcomes. Without rigorous independent oversight, there is a risk that providers will prioritise easy-to-certify skills over more complex but valuable competencies, artificially inflating success rates while failing to improve real employability outcomes.

4. **Participant Satisfaction**

The participant satisfaction KPI requires that at least 75% of trainees evaluate the programme positively. This indicator seeks to capture learner feedback and provide insight into training quality from the perspective of participants.

An important advantage of this KPI is that it offers immediate feedback on training experiences, helping providers identify issues related to course structure, teaching quality, and learning environments. It also acknowledges the role of student engagement in effective learning, as motivated and satisfied participants are more likely to complete training successfully.

Despite these benefits, satisfaction surveys are highly subjective and do not necessarily correlate with training effectiveness or employment outcomes. A participant may rate a programme highly due to engaging instructors or user-friendly materials, even if the training does not lead to meaningful job opportunities.

Moreover, this KPI is vulnerable to manipulation, as providers may offer incentives for positive evaluations or make superficial improvements to training delivery without addressing core issues related to skills development or labour market alignment.

5. **Employer Satisfaction**

The employer satisfaction KPI requires that at least 75% of employers engaged in training must provide a positive evaluation. This indicator aims to ensure that training aligns with industry needs, promoting stronger collaboration between training providers and employers.

One of its main strengths is that it encourages employers to participate in shaping training curricula, making vocational programmes more responsive to labour market demands. Employers who are satisfied with the quality of training are more likely to hire programme graduates, increasing the chances of successful job placements.

However, this KPI has a limited scope, as not all training programmes involve direct employer participation. Many vocational courses provide general skills that may be applicable across multiple industries, making employer feedback less relevant in some cases.

Furthermore, the success of this KPI depends heavily on sufficient response rates from employers. If a significant portion of employers do not participate in the satisfaction survey, the resulting data may provide only a partial view of training effectiveness. Policymakers could consider introducing incentives or streamlined feedback processes-such as simplified online surveys, reminders, or recognition for companies with consistent feedback submission-to boost employer engagement.

Finally, employer satisfaction does not guarantee skill acquisition. A positive rating may be based on general impressions rather than rigorous assessments of trainees' competencies. Without objective measures of workplace performance, employer satisfaction remains a subjective and inconsistent indicator of training effectiveness.

The strengths and weaknesses of these KPIs, which can be classified into four categories, are summarised in Table 4.1. These categories include Labour Impact KPIs, which measure employment outcomes; Programme Output KPIs, which assess certification and completion rates; User Experience KPIs, which reflect participant satisfaction with training; and Employer Outcome KPIs, which capture employer perspectives on training effectiveness.

Table 4.1. Overview of key performance indicators (KPIs) for provider evaluation

Classification, strengths and weaknesses of proposed KPIs

KPI Category	Indicator	Target	Strengths	Weaknesses
Labour Impact KPIs	1. Employment Rate	At least 50% of unemployed trainees must secure employment within 12 months of programme completion.	• Directly assesses employability • Simple to communicate to stakeholders.	• Highly dependent on external labour market conditions. • Focuses on short-term employment.
	2. Job Retention	At least 90% of trained workers must remain employed for at least 12 months.	• Evaluates employment sustainability • Assesses long-term impact.	• Does not account for circumstances out of the control of the employee • Does not account for career progression or skill utilisation. • Influenced by sector-specific trends.
Programme Output KPIs	3. Certification Rate	At least 80% of trainees who complete the programme must obtain certification.	• Encourages completion of training. • Ensures formal skill recognition.	• Certification does not guarantee employability. • Risk of prioritising easier certifications.
User Experience KPIs	4. Participant Satisfaction	At least 75% of trainees must evaluate the programme positively.	• Provides immediate feedback. • Captures learner perception of quality.	• Subjective and may not reflect actual employment outcomes. • Risk of manipulation for higher ratings.
Employer Outcome KPIs	5. Employer Satisfaction	For employer-linked training, at least 75% of employers must provide a positive evaluation.	• Ensures training aligns with industry needs. • Encourages employer engagement.	• Not all programmes involve employers. • Satisfaction may not reflect actual skill acquisition.

Challenges in implementing KPI metrics

The following challenges underscore some of the most pressing concerns arising from the reliance on KPI-driven accountability in the “Jobs Again” reform. Although the indicators themselves-covering employment outcomes, certification rates, and participant and employer satisfaction-can help enhance transparency and provider accountability, certain limitations have surfaced.

1. Over-Reliance on External Labour Market Factors

One of the most significant challenges is the over-reliance on external labour market factors in assessing provider performance. Employment and job retention KPIs depend on variables beyond the control of training providers, including regional disparities, sector-specific demand fluctuations, and broader economic conditions. For instance, providers in high-unemployment regions may face structural challenges that limit job opportunities, making it difficult for training providers to meet employment and retention targets despite offering high-quality training. Similarly, industries with cyclical or seasonal hiring patterns, such as tourism or agriculture, often experience fluctuating employment levels may struggle to meet these targets despite offering high-quality training. This creates a misalignment where funding and accreditation decisions are based on outcomes that providers cannot directly influence.

2. Selection Bias: Incentives to Prioritise Easier-to-Place Trainees

Another key issue is selection bias, which arises from the way performance thresholds are set. Since providers are evaluated based on employment and retention rates, there is an inherent incentive to prioritise trainees who are easier to place in jobs, such as those with higher educational backgrounds or recent work experience. This could lead to the exclusion of individuals most in need of training, such as long-term unemployed workers, migrants, or those with disabilities, thereby reinforcing existing inequalities rather than addressing them. If training providers focus on meeting KPI targets rather than on ensuring access for disadvantaged groups, the reform risks narrowing opportunities rather than expanding them.

3. Limitations of Satisfaction-based Metrics

The use of satisfaction-based metrics presents another challenge. While participant and employer satisfaction KPIs aim to capture feedback on training quality, they are inherently subjective and do not necessarily reflect actual skill acquisition or labour market relevance. A training programme may receive high satisfaction scores due to engaging instructors or a well-structured curriculum, yet fail to improve employment outcomes. Additionally, satisfaction surveys can be influenced by incentives, superficial improvements, or inconsistencies in data collection, making them an unreliable basis for provider evaluation. A more meaningful approach would involve structured pre- and post-training skill assessments to measure actual learning progression rather than relying solely on perception-based indicators.

4. Rigid Pass/Fail Criteria and Short-term Compliance Risks

A further concern is the rigid three-out-of-five failure threshold for removing providers from the registry, which presents a potential risk to training quality and labour market alignment. While intended to ensure provider accountability, the system's reliance on numerical targets over qualitative assessments might lead to a focus on short-term compliance rather than meaningful improvements in training effectiveness. Providers may prioritise meeting statistical thresholds over investing in pedagogical innovation or addressing skill gaps in a sustainable way.

5. Failure to Account for Context-Specific Training Models

Additionally, the binary pass/fail nature of the criteria fails to consider context-specific factors. For instance, upskilling programmes for already employed individuals may focus on improving job performance, career progression, or adapting to new technologies, rather than leading to an immediate job change. The current framework does not adequately accommodate such cases, treating all training programmes under the same rigid structure, which may discourage providers from offering specialised upskilling or lifelong learning opportunities.

Moreover, progression to more advanced vocational programmes could also be recognised as a key indicator of success, particularly for participants with low initial skill levels. Many individuals lack the foundational skills necessary to enrol in job-ready vocational training programmes. In such cases, basic skills training-such as literacy, numeracy, or general education certificates-functions as a critical stepping stone toward employability. Rather than assessing these programmes solely on immediate employment outcomes, advancement to the next stage of education or training should be considered a measure of success.

Without recognising this progression metric, the current system risks undervaluing an essential component of workforce development and inadvertently discouraging investment in foundational skills training for the most disadvantaged learners.

6. Broader Concerns with the Outcome-based Education (OBE) Model

Finally, the broader debate surrounding Outcome-based Education (OBE) raises questions about the long-term impact of this approach. While OBE prioritises measurable employment outcomes, critics argue that this model can oversimplify learning, overlook critical thinking and adaptability, and lead to a narrow focus on test-based performance (Hussey and Smith, 2002[1]). The absence of strong empirical evidence on OBE's effectiveness at scale further complicates its role in vocational training reform. While OBE can be valuable when integrated into a comprehensive quality assurance framework, its limitations must be carefully managed to avoid reducing training effectiveness to a set of rigid employment statistics.

Dimension 5: Co-ordination and Governance

A key structural change introduced by the "Jobs Again" reform is the addition of a new quality assurance layer under DYPA's oversight. Currently, the initial screening of training providers is carried out by EOPPEP, under the Ministry of Education, which evaluates providers based on national accreditation standards. The reform, however, introduces additional quality requirements, including ISO 9001 (Quality Management) and ISO 27001 (Data Security) certifications, as well as performance-based criteria that providers must meet to remain in DYPA's registry.

While these additional requirements serve DYPA's objective of ensuring that training leads to employability, they also fragment the existing quality assurance system by creating a dual-layered accreditation structure. Providers must first meet the Ministry of Education's accreditation criteria and then comply with DYPA's supplementary standards, which include both upfront eligibility requirements and ongoing performance evaluations.

The existence of parallel quality control mechanisms – one under the Ministry of Education through EOPPEP and another introduced by DYPA – creates a dual system of oversight that poses significant governance challenges. These include risks related to co-ordination, regulatory clarity, and institutional alignment. DYPA's efforts to establish its own quality standards, including the implementation of ISO requirements, reflect a strong commitment to accountability. However, without effective co-ordination with EOPPEP, this approach risks generating overlapping responsibilities, divergent benchmarks, and inconsistencies in quality assurance practices.

The duplication of accreditation criteria and quality standards not only increases administrative complexity but also creates uncertainty for training providers navigating the system. Providers have expressed strong concerns that managing two distinct QA frameworks would be burdensome and difficult, particularly for smaller institutions. This added complexity could discourage participation, ultimately reducing the diversity of training provision. To maintain coherence and ensure the success of the reform, it will be essential to align DYPA's standards with the existing national framework and avoid fragmentation of the CVET quality assurance landscape.

Reference

Hussey, T. and P. Smith (2002), "The Trouble with Learning Outcomes", *Active Learning in Higher Education*, Vol. 3/3, pp. 220-233, https://doi.org/10.1177/1469787402003003003. [1]

5 International case studies: Lessons for Greece

This chapter presents international case studies – France, Singapore, Austria, and Estonia – to inform Greece's ILA and CVET reforms. Analysed through the five-dimension framework, the cases highlight diverse quality assurance models, with strong provider accreditation and labour market alignment but limited use of performance-based funding. Lessons from these systems offer practical insights for improving training relevance, oversight, and governance in Greece.

An initial desk-based review of 19 countries and regions,[1] some of which currently operate individual learning accounts (ILA) while others have comparable systems or are in the process of implementing an ILA model, reveals that performance-based funding is rarely used as a primary quality assurance mechanism. Instead, most countries focus on provider accreditation, upfront licensing, and certification requirements to regulate training quality.

Among the countries examined, the most common quality control measures include strict accreditation frameworks for providers, sector-based certification requirements for ILA participation, and additional eligibility criteria for accessing ILA subsidies. These measures often aim to ensure alignment with national workforce priorities, employer partnerships, independent quality audits, and compliance with specific pedagogical standards.

Among the most mature and well-regulated ILA systems, France and Singapore stand out as leading examples. Both countries have developed comprehensive regulatory frameworks that ensure ILA-funded training aligns closely with national skills strategies, employer needs, and lifelong learning objectives. Their models incorporate rigorous accreditation processes, sector-specific validation mechanisms, and ongoing oversight, setting high benchmarks for quality assurance in ILAs.

France and Singapore offer two distinct but complementary approaches that provide valuable insights for Greece's ILA system. France's Compte Personnel de Formation (CPF) model emphasises strong accreditation mechanisms, mandatory certification standards, and transparent enrolment processes, ensuring that only high-quality providers receive public funding. This structured yet flexible system balances learner autonomy with robust quality controls. Singapore, on the other hand, integrates data-driven policymaking, employer collaboration, and long-term impact assessments, ensuring that training remains closely aligned with labour market needs. Its focus on work-based learning and rigorous outcome tracking highlights the benefits of linking training programmes to real employment outcomes. By drawing on these models, Greece can enhance quality assurance, improve labour market alignment, and strengthen the accountability of its ILA system.

In addition to France and Singapore, Austria and Estonia have been included as case studies. Austria's approach emphasises practical skills acquisition through its dual education system, supported by comprehensive accreditation processes and industry collaboration. Estonia, while in the early stages of implementing a comprehensive ILA system, offers insights into aligning vocational training with labour market forecasts and enhancing digital infrastructure for monitoring training outcomes.

These case studies – France, Singapore, Austria, and Estonia – will be analysed using the five-dimension framework presented earlier, allowing for a structured comparison of best practices, challenges, and policy approaches.

Case study 1: Singapore

Singapore has developed one of the most comprehensive and data-driven adult learning systems, ensuring alignment with labour market needs while measuring training effectiveness through structured performance indicators. The SkillsFuture initiative lies at the heart of Singapore's approach, integrating financial incentives, policy interventions, and public-private collaboration to facilitate lifelong learning and workforce adaptability. The SkillsFuture Credit provides funding for individuals aged 25 and above to undertake subsidised training courses, while SkillsFuture Mid-Career Enhanced Subsidies support career transitions in response to evolving industry demands. While many countries incorporate data into policy decisions, Singapore distinguishes itself through the systematic and centralised use of data-driven policymaking, systematically monitoring the labour market impact of training through performance-based tracking mechanisms.

Ensuring Minimum Standards

The SkillsFuture Singapore (SSG) agency is responsible for accrediting and registering training providers, ensuring only high-quality institutions deliver publicly funded training (SkillsFuture, 2022[1]; SkillsFuture, 2024[2]). This involves a structured approach, starting with organisation registration, followed by course accreditation, and then continuous monitoring and quality assurance. At the heart of this process is the Singapore Workforce Skills Qualifications (WSQ) framework, one of the most advanced skills frameworks globally. The WSQ system allows Singapore to align training with industry needs in a highly standardised and effective way, ensuring learners acquire competencies that are both relevant and transferable (Training Partners Gateway, n.d.[3]).

To become a Registered Training Provider (RTP), organisations must first go through an Organisation Registration (OR) process. To be eligible, they must be legally established as a registered entity in Singapore, such as with the Accounting and Corporate Regulatory Authority (ACRA) or the Registry of Societies. Additionally, they need to show they have at least one year of training and education experience, with a record of running courses at least four times in the previous year. The qualifications of trainers and curriculum developers are also evaluated, with key certifications like the Advanced Certificate in Training and Assessment (ACTA) or the Advanced Certificate in Learning and Performance (ACLP) serving as benchmarks of instructional competence.

Following registration, providers can apply for course accreditation under the WSQ system, which ensures that course content aligns with national competency frameworks outlining the skills required across different industries (Singapore Ministry of Education, 2022[4]).

The WSQ's modular and flexible structure allows learners to gain Statements of Attainment as they progress through individual modules, which can be built up towards full qualifications. Providers must develop thorough assessment strategies that effectively evaluate learners' competencies, ensuring that training outcomes meet industry standards. Throughout the accreditation period, compliance with SSG's quality standards is compulsory, with regular audits and feedback mechanisms in place to maintain consistency and relevance.

Ongoing monitoring and quality assurance are essential to maintaining high training standards. The Training Provider Quality Assurance framework provides a comprehensive assessment of each RTP, ensuring that providers adopt systematic approaches to course delivery and maintain sound governance practices. Regular evaluations and trainee feedback are used to assess both instructional effectiveness and learner satisfaction, enabling continuous improvement.

Ensuring Student Participation in Quality Learning

Singapore places a strong emphasis on transparency in course selection and career guidance, ensuring that learners can access relevant training. The SkillsFuture portal provides a centralised platform where individuals can search for subsidised programmes, assess course relevance, and receive career transition guidance. In addition, the government partners with public employment services to direct unemployed or at-risk workers towards suitable training options.

Notably, the SkillsFuture portal also includes channels for participant feedback or complaints, enabling learners to raise concerns if training experiences fail to meet expected standards. This structured approach ensures that substandard providers can be flagged for further review, thereby safeguarding participants and maintaining overall training quality.

A key feature of Singapore's system is its integration of training with employment, allowing individuals to reskill while remaining in the workforce. The Career Conversion Programmes (CCP) have supported

36 000 workers between 2019 and 2023, with 50% of participants aged 40 and above transitioning to long-term job roles in sectors with growth potential.

Mid-career workers benefit from the SkillsFuture Work-Study Programme (WSP), which enables graduates from polytechnics and the Institute of Technical Education (ITE) to gain higher qualifications while acquiring work experience. Studies indicate that Work-Study graduates experience wage premiums of 9-11% compared to peers who enter the workforce directly, with these advantages persisting over several years. This model demonstrates how work-integrated learning contributes to long-term career progression and wage growth.

Measuring Training Outcomes and Long-term Impact

Singapore actively monitors and evaluates training effectiveness through structured post-training mechanisms. The SkillsFuture Career Transition Programme (SCTP) tracks job placement rates as a key measure of success. Since its launch in April 2022, 5 000 trainees have participated, with 54% securing new employment, demonstrating the programme's effectiveness in linking training to employability. In 2019, 77% of Singaporean employers reported that SkillsFuture training programmes enabled employees to assume greater responsibilities.

Post-training evaluation is conducted through the Training Quality and Outcomes Measurement (TRAQOM) initiative, which includes two surveys. The first, conducted upon course completion, captures trainees' perceptions of course quality. The second, conducted three months later, assesses the extent to which the course has impacted job performance and career progression.

Singapore also conducts longitudinal studies on the long-term impact of training. The Ministry of Trade and Industry (MTI), in collaboration with SkillsFuture Singapore (SSG), tracks employment records and income levels over extended periods, providing valuable insights into wage progression and job retention trends.

Performance-based Monitoring

While Singapore does not employ punitive funding mechanisms for underperformance, it does integrate performance-based tracking elements to ensure that training remains effective. Instead of penalising providers, the system emphasises assessing training outcomes through labour market success indicators, including:

- Job placement rates, using SkillsFuture Career Transition Programme data to measure training effectiveness.
- Wage increases post-training, with long-term tracking of participants' earnings growth.
- Transition rates into high-growth industries, ensuring that training programmes support national economic priorities.

Co-ordination and Governance

Singapore's approach to co-ordination is characterised by a highly centralised approach, which would be difficult to replicate elsewhere, primarily co-ordinated by SSG, which operated under the Ministry of Education. The SSG collaborated closely with other agencies, such as Workforce Singapore (WSG) under the Ministry of Manpower, and the Economic Development Board (EDB) under the Ministry of Trade and Industry. This integrated framework ensures cohesive policy implementation and reduces redundancy.

Case study 2: France

France's Compte Personnel de Formation (CPF) exemplifies a structured approach to quality assurance in vocational training, ensuring that training programmes align with labour market needs and enhance individual skills. As an integral component of France's national skills strategy, the CPF mandates strict accreditation requirements for training providers and offering a transparent system for learners to access training opportunities. While performance-based funding is not the primary regulatory tool, France upholds training quality through rigorous accreditation standards and recognised certifications to ensure training quality.

Ensuring Minimum Standards

The French Government introduced a national quality reference framework as part of the law of 5 September 2018 (France Compétences, 2019[5]). This framework mandates that all vocational education and training (VET) providers receiving public funds, including those offering CPF-funded courses, obtain Qualiopi certification, which became mandatory on 1 January 2022, for all training providers receiving public funds, including CPF financing. This certification ensures that only high-quality training organisations can offer CPF-funded courses, reinforcing standardised accreditation and eligibility criteria. These include the relevance of the training offer and its alignment with participant needs, the transparency of the information provided to participants, the resources and skills available within the organisation to deliver high-quality training, monitoring and evaluation processes to measure training effectiveness, and a commitment to continuous improvement.

Ensuring Student Participation in Quality Learning

France has developed a transparent and accessible system for individuals to select and enrol in CPF-funded training. The moncompteformation.gouv.fr platform allows users to view their training rights, search for eligible courses, and register directly with accredited providers, ensuring a streamlined course selection process. While no structured pre-training self-assessment mechanisms are explicitly outlined, CPF's emphasis on individual skill development needs ensures that learners are guided toward training opportunities that match their career goals.

Measuring Training Outcomes and Long-term Impact

The CPF system prioritises certification and recognised qualifications as key indicators of training success. Training programmes funded through CPF often lead to formally recognised qualifications, ensuring that the skills acquired are validated and transferable within the labour market. The CPF platform also incorporates user feedback mechanisms, allowing individuals to rate and review training providers, contributing to continuous quality improvement.

While detailed post-training evaluation mechanisms are not extensively documented, the CPF framework places a strong emphasis on transparency and effectiveness. The system plans to introduce more structured quality measures, further enhancing accountability and training impact assessment. This suggests an ongoing commitment to refining training evaluation processes and ensuring that CPF-funded courses deliver meaningful skill development.

Performance-based Monitoring

Like most ILA systems, France does not rely on direct performance-based funding models. The CPF operates primarily through individual training accounts funded by employer contributions and public subsidies. Rather than conditioning funding on employment outcomes, France enforces strict quality assurance through mandatory accreditation. The Qualiopi certification indirectly promotes high performance standards among providers, ensuring that CPF-funded courses meet consistent and rigorous quality benchmarks.

Skill enhancement is measured primarily through the attainment of recognised qualifications and certifications, ensuring that training remains aligned with national workforce needs. Although specific skill progression metrics are not extensively detailed, the integration of training with national qualifications frameworks ensures standardised learning outcomes. This structured approach maintains a high level of initial quality assurance while allowing for learner flexibility in course selection.

To further strengthen trust and safeguard users, France launched a new audit-based quality evaluation process in 2025 for CPF-funded training. This initiative complements existing mechanisms like Qualiopi, where regular and exhaustive evaluations are conducted to ensure that training providers maintain high standards of quality. These evaluations include reviewing educational processes, assessing the quality, conditions and effectiveness of training programmes, and checking a programme's suitability for the participants' career plans. Despite advancements with Qualiopi, challenges such as detecting fraud and addressing deficiencies in certification processes have emerged. The government is actively working to enhance supervision and ongoing evaluation to address these concerns.

Co-ordination and Governance

France's CPF governance framework defines the roles of key institutions involved in its regulation and administration. France Compétences, created in 2018, is responsible for overseeing the CPF and co-ordinating related training systems. It registers eligible training programmes on the CPF platform, and regulates funding distribution, and certification requirements within the CPF framework.

France Compétences is responsible for regulating training standards and managing the national training levy, while the Ministry of Labour defines policy priorities and may offer targeted top-ups via the Public Employment Service. The Caisse des Dépôts et Consignations regulates training quality, administers CPF accounts and operates the digital platform, ensuring financial transactions between learners and training providers. Employers, unions, and industry representatives contribute to CPF governance by identifying skill needs and co-financing training through mechanisms such as *abondements* (top-ups).

Co-ordination across sectors integrates career guidance, training provision, and employment services. Public employment agencies and regional authorities assist jobseekers in selecting CPF-funded courses, while training providers align their offerings with national qualification frameworks. Monitoring and data-sharing mechanisms track CPF participation, attainment, and funding allocation. The CPF's digital platform centralises these data, supporting continuous assessment of training uptake and labour market relevance.

Case study 3: Austria

Ensuring Minimum Standards

To maintain consistency and quality, Austria requires training providers to be accredited by the Austrian Quality Assurance Agency (AQ Austria) and comply with nationally-accepted quality standards, such as ISO 9001 for quality management (Austrian Federal Ministry of Education, n.d.[6]). Quality assurance is maintained through regular evaluations of training providers, focusing on instructor qualifications, teaching methodologies, and learner support services. Providers must demonstrate that their courses are designed and delivered using evidence-based pedagogical approaches, ensuring that learners acquire both theoretical knowledge and practical skills. Digital learning environments are also subject to quality checks, ensuring that online courses meet the same standards as in-person training.

Ensuring Student Participation in Quality Learning

Austria has developed a transparent and accessible system for individuals to select and enrol in ILA-funded training (European Institute of Public Administration, n.d.[7]). The AMS online platform allows users to explore available training options, view eligibility criteria, and register directly with accredited providers. To support informed decision-making, the platform provides detailed information on course content, learning outcomes, and success rates, enabling individuals to choose training that aligns with their career goals.

Pre-training assessments play a key role in ensuring that learners enrol in courses appropriate to their skill levels. Participants are required to complete competency assessments before starting their training, allowing providers to tailor course content to individual needs. This personalised approach enhances learning effectiveness and increases the likelihood of successful outcomes.

Measuring Training Outcomes and Long-term Impact

The Upper Austrian training account tracks some general participation metrics, such as overall participation, demographics, types of training programmes and regional/sector differences in participation. However, concrete key performance indicators (KPIs) such as certification rates seem not to be measured.

Post-training evaluations assess the extent to which participants have improved their skills and advanced their careers. These evaluations are conducted through follow-up surveys, which capture feedback on job placement rates, career progression, and wage increases. Independent assessments are also carried out to validate training effectiveness and identify areas for improvement.

To measure the long-term impact of training, Austria tracks employment outcomes over a three-year period, monitoring job retention rates, income growth, and transitions to higher-skilled roles (Statistics Austria, 2025[8]). This longitudinal approach provides insights into the lasting benefits of vocational training and helps policymakers assess the overall effectiveness of the ILA system.

Performance-based Monitoring

Austria integrates some performance monitoring into its quality assurance framework. Training providers are evaluated based on key performance indicators, including employment rates, job retention, and participant satisfaction. Providers that consistently achieve high outcomes receive priority access to public funding, creating incentives for continuous improvement.

Employment outcomes are assessed through the AMS labour market tracking system, which monitors aspects such as employment status, job retention etc. to evaluate the overall effectiveness of training programmes, without linking these outcomes to specific providers. In some cases, this data is supplemented by self-reported satisfaction feedback, though its collection is limited to specific training schemes and is currently not applied consistently across all training activities and thus does not play a crucial role in funding decisions related to ILAs.

Further information on the exact performance indicators and what the self-reported satisfaction surveys entails is not available.

Co-ordination and Governance

The governance of Austria's ILAs involves multiple ministries and agencies, each with distinct, yet complementary roles (Cedefop, 2024[9]). The Federal Ministry of Labour and Economy oversees the Public Employment Service (AMS), which administers key schemes supporting individuals in accessing training and obtaining vocational qualifications. It also leads Austria's general efforts on creating a robust ILA, based on an interministerial agreement. The Federal Ministry of Education, Science and Research remains responsible mainly for formal adult education, including adult basic education and lifelong guidance initiatives, providing financial support for general adult education, excluding Austria's apprenticeship system.

Social partners, such as the Chamber of Commerce (Wirtschaftskammer) and the Chamber of Labour (Arbeiterkammer), significantly influence adult learning policies as they have autonomy in bargaining and through organised interest groups and involvement in the government of the AMS, provide important input to the ministries. Additionally, these organisations operate their own vocational training institutes – the Wirtschaftsförderungsinstitut (WIFI) and the Berufsförderungsinstitut (BFI), respectively-offering a wide range of continuing vocational education and training (CVET) programmes. At the regional level, the nine federal states (Länder) have established agencies to support job-related lifelong learning, exemplified by the Vienna Employment Promotion Fund (Wiener ArbeitnehmerInnen Förderungsfonds, waff). These regional bodies enjoy considerable autonomy, allowing them to tailor adult learning initiatives to local needs while aligning with national frameworks.

This setup ensures that while the Ministry of Labour and Economy focuses on employment-related training, the Ministry of Education addresses broader educational needs and policies. Co-ordination between these ministries is facilitated through collaborative frameworks and agreements, aiming to align educational offerings with labour market demands. Despite the clear division of responsibilities, there seems to be a concerted effort to prevent overlap and ensure cohesive policy implementation. Regional governments also play a significant role in Austria, possessing autonomy to tailor adult learning initiatives to local needs.

Case study 4: Estonia

Estonia is in the early phases of implementing a comprehensive ILA system. Currently, adult education and lifelong learning are primarily supported through supply-side funding and established institutions. Several aspects of the adult learning system may require further development before a fully operational ILA system can be effectively introduced. As a result, Estonia is focusing on strengthening existing structures to address issues such as unequal participation, alignment with labour market needs and enhanced quality assurance for adult education providers (Cedefop, 2024[10]).

Ensuring Minimum Standards

Estonia has implemented a comprehensive system for accrediting vocational education and training (VET) providers, focusing on quality assurance and alignment with labour market needs (OECD, 2025[11]). The accreditation process is overseen by the Estonian Quality Agency for Higher and Vocational Education (EKKA).

Estonia's quality assurance system is based on the European Quality Assurance in Vocational Education and Training (EQAVET) guidelines, Cedefop recommendations, and the Estonian Lifelong Learning Strategy 2020, which emphasises management culture, self-assessment, staff training, data use, and stakeholder involvement.

VET providers undergo an initial assessment of professional fields in which they want to offer programmes to get accredited. A positive evaluation from the Estonian Quality Agency for Education (HAKA) accredits providers to offer programmes in these disciplines for six years without requiring ex-ante programme evaluation.

As of 2018, Estonia has been moving towards accrediting groups of programmes within a field of education and training, rather than individual programmes. This approach aims to streamline the process and provide more flexibility to providers.

Ensuring Student Participation in Quality Learning

Estonia employs a system to ensure quality in student participation and learning within CVET that uses mechanisms focusing on guidance and appropriate programme selection rather than pre- and post-assessment. This is combined with previously mentioned adherence to course delivery standards through the stringent accreditation process under the Ministry of Education.

A significant portion of VET programmes involve work-based learning such as apprenticeships, thus providing students practical work experiences.

In terms of non-formal courses, Estonia has started to collect data via the JUHAN system but no further information on the type of data and usage of data is publicly available.

Measuring Training Outcomes and Long-term Impact

Estonia's CVET system places significant emphasis on measuring training outcomes and long-term impact, using a combination of certification processes, student feedback, and broader performance-based monitoring mechanisms.

Upon completion of a VET programme, students receive nationally recognised qualifications aligned with the Estonian Qualifications Framework (EQF), ensuring they possess the necessary competencies for specific roles. Student feedback is actively gathered through course evaluations, surveys, and other mechanisms, informing continuous improvements in course content and teaching methods.

Furthermore, Estonia tracks the labour market outcomes of VET graduates, monitoring employment rates and career progression to assess the long-term impact of training. Despite the long-standing policy of paid study leave in Estonia, no statistical data on the use of study leaves and no formal evaluation of their effects are available.

Performance-based Monitoring

Estonia does not conduct specific performance-based monitoring activities.

Training providers of Estonian Training-Related Active Labour Market Policies (ALMPs) must be registered in the Estonian Education Information System EHIS, deliver courses aligned with specified curricula, and engage in monthly reporting to the Estonian Unemployment Insurance Fund. However, detailed information on what these specified curricula entail, or the reporting data are not publicly available.

Co-ordination and Governance

The governance and co-ordination of ILAs in Estonia involve collaboration between key ministries, agencies, and social partners, each with distinct but interconnected responsibilities.

At the national level, the Ministry of Education and Research and the Ministry of Social Affairs share primary responsibility for supporting adult learning. The Ministry of Education and Research is responsible for ensuring the quality and accessibility of educational opportunities, including both formal and non-formal learning. Meanwhile, the Ministry of Social Affairs, through the Estonian Unemployment Insurance Fund (EUIF), identifies target groups that would benefit from further education and provides financial support for training.

Collaboration between ministries is complemented by the involvement of key stakeholders such as the Estonian Qualifications Authority (Kutsekoda) and OSKA, the national system for anticipating future skill demands. While OSKA's recommendations are binding for the support provided by the EUIF, they remain advisory for initiatives funded by the Ministry of Education and Research, reflecting a balance between centralised guidance and institutional autonomy.

Social partners, including employer organisations and trade unions, play a consultative role in shaping adult learning policies. However, their influence is relatively limited compared to other European Union countries, with collective bargaining and co-ordinated training initiatives being less prevalent. Employers are expected to contribute to workforce upskilling through internal training and financial support for external courses, while individuals are encouraged to take responsibility for their own professional development.

Ongoing efforts to improve co-ordination, expand digital platforms like JUHAN, and enhance the quality assurance framework aim to create a more inclusive and responsive adult learning system in Estonia.

References

Austrian Federal Ministry of Education, S. (n.d.), *Accreditation and quality assurance*, https://www.bmbwf.gv.at/en/Topics/Higher-education---universities/Higher-education-system/HS-QSG.html (accessed on 26 February 2025). [6]

Cedefop (2024), "Individual Learning Accounts: Case Study Austria (Draft)", https://www.cedefop.europa.eu/files/draft_case_study_at_clean.pdf (accessed on 28 August 2025). [9]

Cedefop (2024), *Individual Learning Accounts: Case Study Estonia (Draft)*, https://www.cedefop.europa.eu/files/final_case_ee_formatted_rev_gh_ms_clean.pdf (accessed on 26 February 2025). [10]

European Institute of Public Administration (n.d.), *Introduction of a New AMS Job Search Engine for More Transparency in the Austrian Labour Market*, https://www.eipa.eu/de/epsa/introduction-of-a-new-ams-job-search-engine-for-more-transparency-in-the-austrian-labour-market/ (accessed on 18 August 2025). [7]

France Compétences (2019), *The law on the professional future: the quality requirement*, https://www.francecompetences.fr/fiche/la-loi-avenir-professionnel-lexigence-qualite/ (accessed on 26 February 2025). [5]

OECD (2025), "Ensuring quality in VET and higher education: Getting quality assurance right", *OECD Education Policy Perspectives*, No. 118, OECD Publishing, Paris, https://doi.org/10.1787/812ff006-en. [11]

Singapore Ministry of Education (2022), *SkillsFuture Accreditation*, https://www.moe.gov.sg/news/parliamentary-replies/20221129-skillsfuture-accreditation (accessed on 28 August 2025). [4]

SkillsFuture (2024), *Singapore Agency Terms for Training Providers*, https://www.skillsfuture.gov.sg/docs/default-source/resources/terms-conditions/ssg_term_for_tps_010324_rpd_v01final21d3a692-b7c6-4d0a-82ee-af1e28806afa.pdf (accessed on 26 February 2025). [2]

SkillsFuture (2022), *Singapore Agency Terms for Training Providers*, https://www.skillsfuture.gov.sg/docs/default-source/resources/terms-conditions/ssg_tp-tc_17102022_rpd_v01final.pdf (accessed on 28 August 2025). [1]

Statistics Austria (2025), "Monitoring of Education-Related Employment Behaviour", https://www.statistik.at/fileadmin/announcement/2025/01/20250128BibErEN.pdf (accessed on 26 February 2025). [8]

Training Partners Gateway (n.d.), *Organisation Registration for First-Time Training Providers*, https://www.tpgateway.gov.sg/plan-courses/organisation-registration-for-first-time-training-provider/apply-for-organisation-registration (accessed on 26 February 2025). [3]

Note

[1] Austria (Upper Austria); Croatia; Cyprus; Estonia; France; Germany; Greece; Ireland; Italy (Tuscany); Latvia; Lithuania; Malta; Netherlands; Poland; Romania; Scotland (United Kingdom); Singapore; Slovak Republic; United States (Michigan & Washington).

6 Conclusions and recommendations for refining the "Jobs Again" reform

This chapter summarises the assessment of Greece's "Jobs Again" reform and presents targeted recommendations across five key dimensions. While the reform strengthens accountability – particularly through the introduction of KPIs and a registry of training providers – challenges remain in ensuring the relevance of training, improving governance and institutional co-ordination, and promoting equity. Recommendations include harmonising accreditation systems, strengthening learner feedback and pre-training assessment mechanisms, refining the use of KPIs, and improving co-ordination among responsible agencies.

This report has assessed the *"Jobs Again"* reform, focusing on its quality assurance mechanism. The reform represents a significant shift towards performance-based accountability in Greece's vocational training system, introducing a structured registry of eligible providers and key performance indicators (KPIs) to measure training outcomes. These measures aim to improve training quality, align education with labour market needs, and ensure public funds are directed towards effective programmes.

The reform introduces several positive changes, including a stronger focus on employability outcomes, enhanced provider accountability, and a digital platform to facilitate training access and monitoring. The use of employment and job retention rates as KPIs reinforces the objective of ensuring training leads to real workforce integration. Additionally, requiring providers to meet ISO quality standards adds another layer of assurance that training institutions maintain high delivery standards. The introduction of individual learning accounts (ILAs) also grants learners more autonomy in selecting courses, promoting lifelong learning and career adaptability.

However, several challenges remain, particularly in ensuring training relevance, refining performance evaluation, enhancing flexibility, and improving provider accountability mechanisms. The reliance on post-training employment metrics does not guarantee that training content aligns with labour market needs, and the absence of a structured pre-training assessment makes it difficult to measure actual skills progression. Additionally, the dual-layered quality assurance system under DYPA (Greece's Public Employment Service) and EOPPEP (National Organisation for the Certification of Qualifications and Vocational Guidance) risks fragmenting oversight and increasing administrative burdens.

This section outlines key recommendations that could help refine the reform, making it more adaptable, equitable, and results-driven. Each recommendation is mapped to one of the five dimensions introduced earlier-Ensuring Minimum Standards, Ensuring Student Participation in Quality Learning, Measuring Training Outcomes and Long-term Impact, Performance-based Monitoring, and Co-ordination and Governance-so that the guidance directly addresses the distinct areas of improvement identified in the analysis.

Dimension 1: Ensuring Minimum Standards

Recommendation 1.1: Operate a Unified System of Accreditation for Initial Accreditation of Education Organisations

A key issue in the current reform is the fragmentation of quality assurance mechanisms due to the dual-layered accreditation system between EOPPEP (under the Ministry of Education, Religious Affairs and Sport) and DYPA (under the Ministry of Labour and Social Security).

Currently, EOPPEP oversees the initial accreditation of training providers, setting the baseline for participation in publicly funded programmes. The "Jobs Again" reform introduces additional quality requirements under DYPA, including ISO certifications and performance-based KPIs to remain in the registry. While these measures aim to enhance training relevance and accountability, they create overlapping responsibilities, regulatory inconsistencies, and increased administrative burdens for providers.

Similar to Singapore's single accreditation process under SkillsFuture Singapore (SSG) and France's Qualiopi certification, Greece should consolidate its accreditation requirements into a single, coherent framework. This would eliminate overlapping responsibilities between DYPA and EOPPEP, reducing confusion for training providers and improving regulatory clarity.

Leveraging DYPA's digital platform, the accreditation process should be digitised to enable real-time data sharing between regulatory bodies, training providers, and employers. This integration would support more efficient monitoring, reduce administrative delays, and ensure that quality assurance processes are transparent and accessible.

Recommendation 1.2: Improve the Use of ISO Standards in Accreditation Procedures

ISO standards can play a valuable role in the accreditation of adult learning providers, as seen in Austria and Germany. However, their effective application requires careful selection of the appropriate standard and the establishment of clear guidance mechanisms to ensure alignment with policy objectives. While ISO 9001 is widely used as a general-purpose quality management system, it primarily focuses on customer satisfaction rather than educational effectiveness or labour market relevance. As a result, high participant satisfaction may not necessarily indicate alignment with national workforce strategies or government priorities.

To better address the specific needs of training providers, Greece could consider alternative ISO standards that offer a more tailored approach to educational quality assurance. For instance, ISO 21001 – Educational Organisation Management Systems is designed specifically for formal education and training institutions, helping them integrate pedagogical principles, learner-centred approaches, and structured quality management. It focuses on improving institution-wide processes, ensuring that learning objectives, teaching methodologies, and assessment practices align with recognised educational standards.

For non-formal education and vocational training, ISO 29990 provides a framework tailored to training providers operating outside the formal education system, such as adult learning centres and vocational training institutes. It emphasises learning outcomes, competence development, and learner satisfaction, ensuring that non-formal training meets industry and employment requirements. Complementing this, ISO 29993 applies to specific learning services rather than entire training organisations, focusing on programme design, learner engagement, and performance evaluation. This ensures that individual courses – whether in professional development, corporate training, or short-term vocational programmes – meet quality and effectiveness standards.

Dimension 2: Ensuring Student Participation in Quality Learning

Recommendation 2.1: Introducing a Learner Complaints Alert System

Ensuring the quality of training programmes is essential for the credibility and effectiveness of individual learning accounts (ILA). One of the key principles of the European Quality Assurance in Vocational Education and Training (EQAVET) framework is the integration of learner feedback mechanisms to drive continuous improvement. EQAVET encourages VET providers to implement systems that allow learners to provide feedback and lodge complaints.

To enhance accountability, a learner complaints and alert system could be embedded within the ILA digital platform, enabling trainees to submit feedback and to report substandard training experiences. This system should support anonymous and confidential submissions, categorise complaints based on severity, and require time-bound responses from training providers. A high volume of complaints or unresolved issues could lead to corrective actions, temporary suspension, or removal from the approved provider list. This mechanism would not only reinforce quality assurance but also protect learners from ineffective or misleading training programmes.

A notable reference point is Singapore's SkillsFuture programme, where participants and employers can submit detailed feedback-including complaints-directly through the official SkillsFuture website. Although not a real-time "alert mechanism," this structured feedback channel enables the authorities to investigate allegations of substandard training, conduct quality audits, and, if necessary, revoke approval for non-compliant providers. In practice, this means that training institutions are held accountable for any negative learner experiences. The system also maintains a publicly accessible record of provider ratings, enabling prospective learners to make more informed enrolment decisions.

If Greece were to adapt this model, integrating the complaints alert mechanism directly into the ILA platform could enhance its effectiveness. Instead of relying on manual reviews, this approach would enable real-time scrutiny of providers in response to complaints.

Dimension 3: Measuring Training Outcomes and Long-term Impact

Recommendation 3.1: Implement Pre-training Questionnaires as Part of the Enrolment Process

Performance evaluation should extend beyond employment and certification rates to measure actual skills acquisition and application. The current reform focuses primarily on post-training employment indicators without considering participants' initial skill levels or the specific learning gains achieved through training. Greece could implement a pre-post training evaluation framework that assesses skills before and after training. This approach, inspired by Singapore's TRAQOM system, would provide policymakers and providers with objective data on training effectiveness.

Two models for pre-training assessments exist. In the first, a baseline assessment could help establish participants' initial skill levels, ensuring that they receive training at the appropriate level and that the impact of training can be accurately measured. Greece could develop standardised assessment tools to evaluate initial level of skills.

The second approach is to monitor achievement of learning objectives by using skill self-assessments and/or learning objective questionnaires in the pre-training phase, and quizzing participants on their perceived progress at the end of the training. Implementing a similar approach in Greece could help ensure that training content, duration, and intensity are aligned with participants' actual needs.

Recommendation 3.2: Administer Training Questionnaires Centrally

Training questionnaires should be integrated into the future digital platform for training. Pre-training questionnaires should be administered as part of the enrolment process on a centralised online portal. Post-training questionnaires should also be administered not by the providers, but centrally via the portal. To ensure completion of such questionnaires it is recommended to oblige providers to upload final assessment results/certifications to the portal. Learners would then be required to complete the questionnaire to retrieve the grade or certificate. This would achieve twin objectives of firstly ensuring that all students participate in evaluation, and secondly limiting providers from exercising undue influence on the evaluation process.

Dimension 4: Performance-based Monitoring

Recommendation 4.1: Expand the KPI Framework to Enhance Flexibility

The current rigid five-KPI model could be expanded, allowing providers more flexibility in meeting performance expectations. A weighted scoring system would allow providers to meet a combination of KPIs rather than applying the same benchmarks universally. This would help account for differences in regional labour markets, industry-specific hiring patterns, and the challenges faced by providers working with vulnerable populations.

In Austria, the performance evaluation of training providers incorporates a weighted system that considers various factors such as regional employment rates and participant demographics. This approach ensures that providers working in challenging environments or with disadvantaged populations are assessed fairly, acknowledging the additional efforts required to achieve positive outcomes.

The Greek system could introduce differentiated performance criteria based on regional unemployment levels, economic sectors, and target populations. Providers working with long-term unemployed individuals, migrants, or those with lower employability prospects should have alternative benchmarks, recognising the additional challenges in securing job placements. Potential indicators are shown in Table 6.1.

Table 6.1. Expanded performance indicators for training effectiveness

Expanding performance metrics to capture workforce impact and accessibility

KPI Category	Indicator	Description
Labour Impact KPIs	Wage Increase	Percentage of participants reporting an increase in average income after completing the programme.
	Transition to Formal Employment	Percentage of graduates securing stable jobs with formal contracts and benefits.
	Internal Promotions	Percentage of employees who receive promotions within their current roles after training.
Programme Quality KPIs	Completion Rate	Percentage of participants successfully completing their training programmes with full attendance.
User Experience KPIs	Skills Improvement Perception	Percentage of participants reporting an improvement in their professional skills after training.
	Programme Accessibility	Percentage of participants who consider the programmes accessible in terms of cost, location, and scheduling.
	Complaints Incidence	Proportion of training participants lodging formal complaints about programme quality or relevance, indicating potential shortfalls in course delivery or alignment with participants' needs.
Employer Outcome KPIs	Collaboration with the Private Sector	Number of programmes co-designed with employers or key sectors.
	Internship or Work Placement Participation	Proportion of programmes offering internships or practical experiences as part of the training.
	Employer perception of skill improvement	Employer perception of soft-skills, competences and attitude improvements
Broadening Participation and Accessibility KPIs (new category)	Access for Disadvantaged Groups	Percentage of participants from vulnerable groups (e.g. women, migrants, persons with disabilities).
	Regional Participation	Participation rate in rural areas, less-developed regions, or areas with higher unemployment rates.

The current "Jobs Again" reform does not foresee regular evaluation and updating of KPIs. As Greece is implementing such a unique and forward-looking reform, it is recommended to establish a periodic review process for the KPI framework to assess its relevance and effectiveness. This should involve stakeholders, including training providers, employers, and policymakers, to gather diverse perspectives and make informed adjustments. This iterative process will help maintain a dynamic and responsive evaluation system.

Finally, all KPIs should be published, giving learners some element of choice in the quality-levels of the institutions with which they wish to pursue a learning opportunity.

Recommendation 4.2: Introduce Incentives for High-Performer Providers

Instead of focusing solely on exclusion mechanisms for underperforming providers, the system could reward training providers that achieve strong, long-term employment outcomes.

High-performing organisations that consistently meet or exceed their performance metrics can receive benefits such as additional funding, public recognition, and promotional opportunities. For instance, the U.S. Department of Labor administers skills training grants through programs like the Critical Sectors Job Quality Grant Program and the Strengthening Community Colleges Training Grants Program, which provide financial support to institutions demonstrating excellence in training delivery (U.S. Department of Labor, 2024[1]). In Austria and Germany, adult learning providers may receive additional resources for courses deemed particularly valuable for societal purposes. Furthermore, extra subsidies are allocated to support staff training and innovation projects, fostering both educational quality and programme development (Cedefop, 2024[2]).

Top-performing providers may additionally be granted greater autonomy in curriculum design and implementation, allowing them to innovate and tailor programmes to specific industry needs. This flexibility can lead to more responsive and effective training solutions.

Instead of imposing strict penalties on providers not meeting certain KPIs, offering targeted support can be more beneficial. This approach includes professional development opportunities, sharing best practices, and providing additional resources to address specific challenges. Such measures foster a culture of continuous improvement and capacity building. This would go in line with the World Bank's recommendation for demand-driven skills training and results-based contracting, emphasising support for training providers to enhance their performance (World Bank, 2020[3]).

Providers which are subject to significant number of complaints, or who consistently rank bottom of the metrics lists, should still have licences withdrawn.

Dimension 5: Co-ordination and Governance

Recommendation 5.1: Ensuring Co-ordination in Quality Assurance

The responsibilities for the delivery and oversight of CVET in Greece is fragmented, with challenges undermining quality assurance and operational oversight. The Ministry of Education oversees formal education and training, while the Ministry of Labour is responsible for non-formal, continuing education and training. Additionally, several other ministries run training initiatives aligned with their respective needs and mandates. This fragmentation is further compounded by the inclusion of training initiatives in applications for European Social Fund (ESF) funding by multiple ministries. This has led to overlapping training schemes with limited co-ordination, creating inefficiencies and reducing the strategic alignment of CVET provision across the country.

A range of non-governmental actors also play a significant role in CVET provision. For instance, organisations such as the Hellenic Federation of Enterprises (SEV) and companies like Cisco have developed small-scale, high-quality training initiatives that address labour market needs. These initiatives are often designed collaboratively with employers, sectoral federations, and private certifiers, ensuring their quality and relevance. Sectoral actors, such as tourism and retail federations under SEV, also provide important contributions by targeting sector-specific skills needs. However, these initiatives remain disconnected from the public training schemes, limiting their scalability and potential impact.

DYPA plays a central role in CVET by supporting and funding training programmes based on an analysis and anticipation of labour market needs. Once participants complete their training, their skills are certified by third-party certifiers. Participants can choose from one to two designated certifiers per programme to validate their skills. Certifiers operate under the Ministry of Development, while EOPPEP (under the Ministry of Education) oversees CVET providers. DYPA also conducts spontaneous audits to ensure programme delivery and compliance with requirements.

A key issue in the current reform is the fragmentation of quality assurance mechanisms due to the dual-layered accreditation system between EOPPEP and DYPA. Currently, EOPPEP oversees the initial accreditation of training providers, setting the baseline for participation in publicly funded programmes. The "Jobs Again" reform introduces additional quality requirements under DYPA, including ISO certifications and performance-based KPIs to remain in the registry. While these measures aim to enhance training relevance and accountability, they risk creating overlapping responsibilities, regulatory inconsistencies, and increased administrative burdens for providers.

Greater co-ordination between DYPA and the Ministry of Education is crucial to ensure that providers are not forced to submit the same information multiple times or meet conflicting sets of criteria. Under the current dual-layer system, training institutions may face duplicative data requests from EOPPEP and DYPA, increasing their administrative workload without adding tangible value to quality assurance. To address this, both agencies should collaborate in developing a shared data infrastructure that captures the full range of quality indicators-such as learner progression, labour market outcomes, and teaching practices-through a single reporting channel. Likewise, as EOPPEP updates its accreditation standards, DYPA should have a seat at the table to align these changes with the performance-based KPIs it oversees, ensuring that no overlap or contradiction arises in reporting requirements, which not only creates inefficiencies but also places an excessive burden on training providers.

Recommendation 5.2: Ensuring Transparency in Certification through a Unified Certifier Selection Process

There are concerns about the reliability of certification outcomes in Greece's CVET landscape, with persistently high pass rates prompting questions about how objectively certain assessments are conducted. To address these worries, DYPA could take a more proactive role in selecting certifiers-for example, by designating a single certifier for each geographic region or occupational sector, chosen through a transparent, competitive process. Under this model, providers would be required to have their trainees certified by the officially designated entity, thus reducing the risk of inflated pass rates. Centralising certifier selection in this way would also standardise quality benchmarks, promote uniform oversight, and uphold the credibility of the certification process. Over time, such an approach could strengthen public confidence in Greece's vocational training system by ensuring that certifications genuinely reflect trainees' acquired skills

Recommendation 5.3: Achieve Full Digitisation of All Processes Through a National Digital Portal

A centralised digital (ILA) platform, jointly managed by DYPA, EOPPEP, and the joint governing body, should serve as the backbone of the co-ordination framework, as recommended by the EU Council Recommendation on Individual Learning Accounts.

Inspired by Singapore's SkillsFuture portal and Estonia's OSKA system this platform should integrate real-time data from training providers, labour market analytics, and performance indicators, enabling seamless information sharing between agencies. The platform should support joint monitoring of provider performance, tracking key metrics such as participant outcomes, participant feedback, certification rates, and employer feedback. Access to performance data should be shared between DYPA, EOPPEP, and the NSC, promoting transparency and facilitating data-driven decision-making. Additionally, the platform could host a shared database of accredited courses, aligned with both national and European qualifications frameworks, ensuring that training providers deliver standardised, transferable skills.